For
Christina, Thanks for being
a great sister.
Love
Staci
12·27·98

A SISTER
is a
SPECIAL FRIEND

By Claudine Gandolfi

Illustrated by Richard Judson Zolan

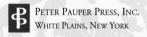
PETER PAUPER PRESS, INC.
WHITE PLAINS, NEW YORK

To Michele,
who is like a sister to me—just kidding.

Artist: Richard Judson Zolan
Illustrations copyright ©1998
Art Licensing Properties, LLC.

Book design by Mullen & Katz

Text copyright © 1998
Peter Pauper Press, Inc.
202 Mamaroneck Avenue
White Plains, NY 10601
All rights reserved
ISBN 0-88088-899-7
Printed in China
7 6 5 4 3 2 1

Introduction

$$\sim$$

*Y*ou have been given a very precious gift, a sister. You may have begged to have a sister. You may have wished to be an only child. Whatever the circumstances were, be grateful for this very special person who has enriched your life, perhaps more than you know. Think of all the times when she came to your defense or cheered you up. Think of the times when she was able to tell you something when your friends couldn't. Recall all the silly secrets you fought about. Most of all, remember to tell her that you love her.

—C. G.

A Sister is a Special Friend

Your sister is a gift from above.

~

Your sister will surely remember
all the special moments that have
occurred in your lives, whether you
want her to or not.

Sometimes it's hard to recall that your sister is not meant to be your carbon copy.

~

When following in your sister's footsteps make sure to make your own tracks.

A knowing look
between sisters
can carry
the weight of
a thousand
words.

Your sister is a built-in friend.

~

To a sister,
a locked diary is all the invitation
she needs.

A Sister is a Special Friend

When you've grown up together, you *know* what your sister is thinking.

~

Even if she's not near, you can always hear your sister's voice giving advice, congratulating you, reprimanding you, caring for you.

A Sister is a Special Friend

No matter what happens between you and your sister, you know she'll always be there for you in times of need.

~

For each of the "borrowed" clothes that were ruined, there is a moment of joy that evens things out.

A Sister is a Special Friend

Your sister will always come to your defense no matter what's happened between you.

There is an inherent understanding between sisters that stems not only from being related, but also from being raised together.

*N*o matter
how many years
separate you and your sister,
there is no
generation gap
between you.

A Sister is a Special Friend

Some sisters look as different as night
and day, while others can pass for twins.
What really makes you sisters
is on the inside.

~

Watching your sister accomplish
something creates a joy within you,
as if you had been the one to succeed.

Teasing, sharing, snitching, protecting, quarreling, and supporting come with the territory.

No two sisters act exactly the same toward each other. That's what makes each relationship special.

A Sister is a Special Friend

No matter how old you are, your sister can reduce you to acting like a child or encourage you to your full adult potential.

❧

Step-, half-, adopted-, are all useless additions . . . what matters is that you are sisters!

When seen through loving eyes, there is no "prettier," "smarter," "friendlier," "favorite" sister. Each sister possesses her own inner worth.

Competitiveness with your sister leads
to a greater understanding of yourself.

~

Nothing can compare to the closeness
sisters share. It is a warm hug
when needed most.

*I*f you
held grudges
against your sister,
where would you
put them all?

A sister
will be there for you
l-o-n-g after
your friends
have gone.

Sisters should
never try to
outshine each other.
Find your unique talent
and triumph in that.

Sibling rivalry sometimes
occurs between sisters.
It's difficult not to bruise a few egos
when you're fashioning who you are
as a person.

Perhaps you
can realize how great
your sister is
only when she is absent
from your life.

*W*hen sisters
share their
innermost thoughts,
they strengthen
the bond that
they were born with.

*T*hat shared bedroom
you had as children,
which may have been a source
of frustration, will be the
root of many beautiful and
humorous memories.

A Sister is a Special Friend

You don't have to
try to cover up your hurts, fears,
and disappointments.
To your sister, your "best face"
is the one that
truly matches your mood.

*Y*our sister is
your first confidante,
your first best friend,
your first rival,
and your first champion.

Older sisters
can function as
second mothers—nurturing,
guiding, teaching—whether
you want them to
or not.

You may have been amazed
at what your younger sister
"got away with" when you were kids.
Don't forget that she
had to contend not only with
your mother but also with you.

In your sister, you see a reflection of
yourself. Sometimes it takes skill to see
past the reflection to her true image.

~

That knowing glint in your sister's eye
is a reflection of your shared secrets.

*B*ecause of
the special comfort that
comes with sisterly love,
there is room for frankness
and gentle criticism.

$\mathcal{A}$s you grow older
your sister becomes your best friend.
Gone are the reasons for arguing.
What remains is
the attachment.

*Y*our sister will
never lie to you,
just to tell you what you
want to hear.
Honesty will flow naturally
between you.

A Sister is a Special Friend

*T*hink about
how much your sister means to you,
and you will know how much
you are valued
as well.

The bond between sisters
is more forgiving and elastic than
between the closest of friends.
Through neglect, long absences, and fights,
sisters still remain sisters.

The song of sisters rises and falls, creating a mellifluous harmony.

~

Your sister won't always agree with what you say, but she'll support your right to say it.

*J*ust as
certain colors go well together,
sisters' personalities
can complement
each other.

A Sister is a Special Friend

Sisters are
an enduring testament
to life's

sweetest moments.

*I*n your sister you can see . . .
your mother's eyes, your uncle's
chin, your father's brow.
Having a sister can be like
having your whole family
with you!